HAUNTED York

compulsion,
supernatural
adjective
understanding or the laws of nature
noun (the supernatural)
adjective
Third Eye Concepts

HAUNTED York

ISBN: 978-0-9555662-0-2

Design, layout & illustration © **Ian Forster**
Research, photography & text © **Vincent Danks**

Printed and bound by **Arti Grafiche Srl.**, Rome, Italy

Published 2007 by

Blue Angel P·R·E·S·S

www.**blueangelpress**.com
www.**hauntedyork**.com

CASTLE MUSEUM
LITTER
CITY OF YORK

Contents

6 Introduction
8 Foreword
10 The York Barguest
12 The Church of Holy Trinity
14 The Yorkshire Museum
16 The Treasurer's House
18 York Theatre Royal
20 College Street
22 York Minster
24 Clifford's Tower
26 Bedern
28 St William's College
30 The Shambles
32 The King's Manor
36 The Castle Museum
38 Haunted Pubs
48 Ghost Walks
50 Information
54 Map
56 Epilogue

An introduction to…

the most haunted city in Europe

While the accuracy of the above accolade may be disputed by other haunted cities in Europe, what cannot be denied is that the sheer volume of documented sightings ranks York as one of the most haunted cities in the world.

Founded in AD 71 the city has continually been regarded as an important military and administrative base, with the consequence of playing host to a number of different invaders. For the Romans, whose ghostly legacy has created one of the best known sightings in the country, York, or Eboracum as they named it, was established and developed as a military strongpoint and excavations of remains, including a bath, temple and Roman bridge are still continuing today.

The Minster, with its variety of manifestations, is England's largest mediaeval cathedral and one of Europe's largest gothic churches. It was originally built in 627, although possibly on a different sight.

In 866 the city fell prey to the invading Vikings, who renamed it Jorvik and ruled the area for nearly a hundred years until expelled by the Anglo-Saxons. The late mediaeval period saw prosperous growth and much of the building work, such as the city walls and their entrance gates (known as 'bars') still survive to this day. The old butcher's street known as 'The Shambles' dates from about the same period and although now home to gift shops rather than meat sellers, it's one of the most atmospheric places in the city.

All the stories in this book are sightings from within the city of York and the locations are marked on the map at the end of the book.
In addition to creating your own 'ghost walk', there are a number of guided walks that are detailed in the information sections at the end of the book.

Happy ghost hunting!

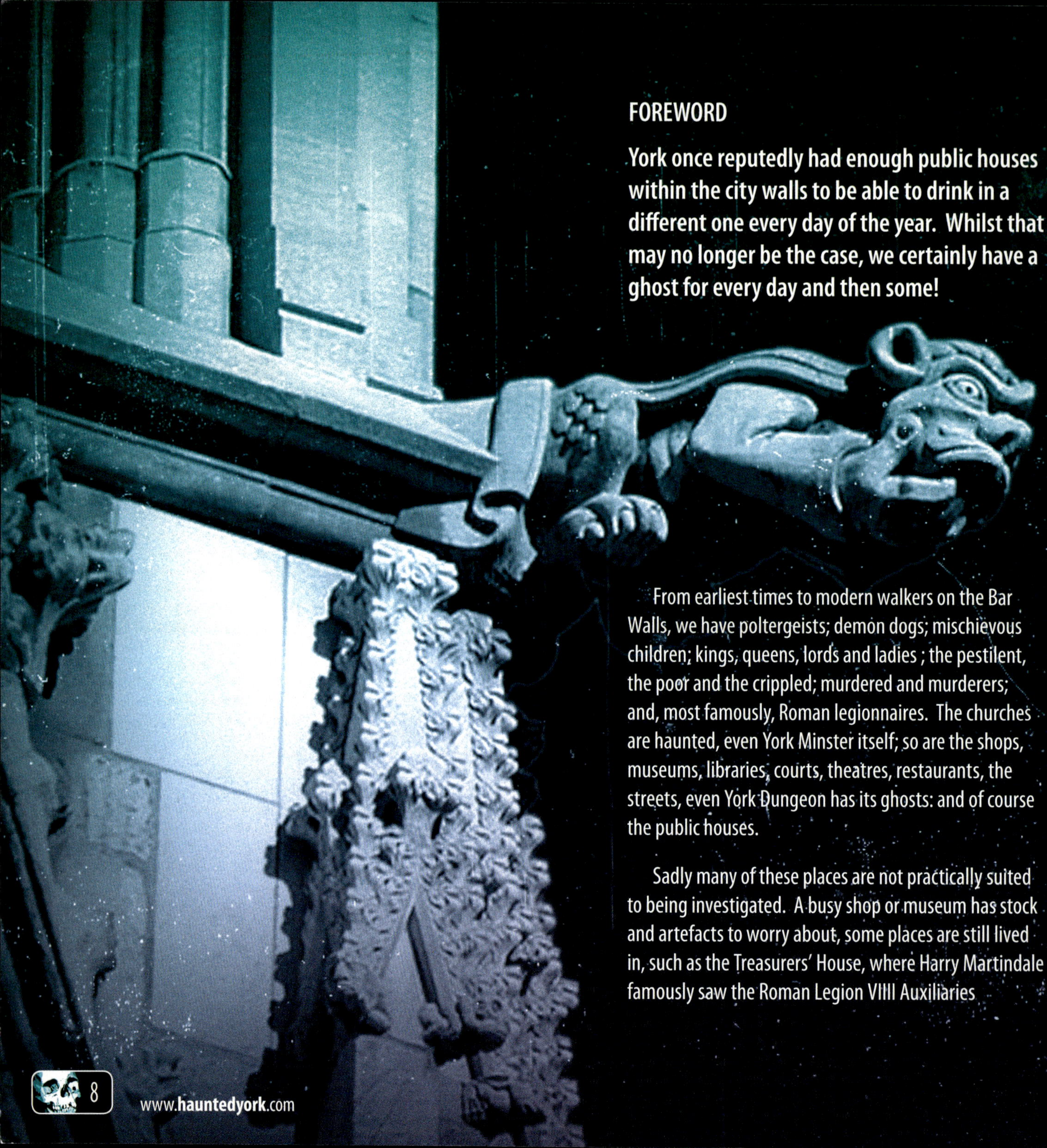

FOREWORD

York once reputedly had enough public houses within the city walls to be able to drink in a different one every day of the year. Whilst that may no longer be the case, we certainly have a ghost for every day and then some!

From earliest times to modern walkers on the Bar Walls, we have poltergeists; demon dogs; mischievous children; kings, queens, lords and ladies ; the pestilent, the poor and the crippled; murdered and murderers; and, most famously, Roman legionnaires. The churches are haunted, even York Minster itself; so are the shops, museums, libraries, courts, theatres, restaurants, the streets, even York Dungeon has its ghosts: and of course the public houses.

Sadly many of these places are not practically suited to being investigated. A busy shop or museum has stock and artefacts to worry about, some places are still lived in, such as the Treasurers' House, where Harry Martindale famously saw the Roman Legion VIIII Auxiliaries trudging through the floor and have no wish to have their peace disturbed further. The King's Manor is now part of the University of York, yet amongst its beautiful stonework there are ghosts aplenty: its own soldiers, this time seventeenth century casualties, along with Henry Hastings, the Earl of Huntingdon; the Black Abbot; Thomas Wentworth, Earl of Strafford and even one of Henry VIII's tragic queens, Catherine Howard.

In many cases, though, a daytime visit can at least give you a feel of the place, and in many cases the hauntings are not restricted to the nighttime. Micklegate Bar is haunted by a young girl, Sarah Brocklebank, who has playfully made her presence felt day or night. Another young girl haunts The Antiques Centre on Stonegate, quite possibly she is Laura Hodgson, the city's Victorian Gas Engineer's daughter: whoever she may be, she has appeared to staff during the day time on more than one occasion. The lecherous George Villiers, 2nd Duke of Buckingham, made his presence felt to the female staff and visitors of the Cock & Bottle on Skeldergate for many years whenever the urge took him, although in recent years reports are few and far between of this groping ghost!

The Eboracum Legion Bathhouse's ghosts do not adhere to the conventional night time hauntings either, with visitors to the museum reporting seeing, hearing and sensing presences; the same is true of the Richard III Museum in Monk Bar.

Further investigation can cast doubt over some of our ghosts, but still more are not easily dismissed, and the competition for most haunted public house is most hotly contested: is it the Golden Fleece with the Lord Mayor's wife, Alice Peckitt, reputedly a visitor from her home next door (known as Lady Peckitt although not a member of the aristocracy, as in York there was a tradition regarding Lord Mayors and their Lady: "He is lord for a year and a day. She is lady for ever and aye"), ghosts seen walking through walls and ominous floating heads? Or is it Ye Olde Starre Inne on Stonegate, haunted by wounded soldiers, black cats and a little old lady; further down the road the Punch Bowl also lays claim to numerous ghosts. Maybe it's the Snickelways on Goodramgate, with a plethora of ghosts including sights, sounds, smells and feelings of innate evil. The hauntings at the York Arms on High Petergate have been documented for many years and, more recently, York Brewery itself has become a centre for paranormal activity.

01

The York Barguest

Although a shape-shifter by nature, the people of the north of England know the Barguest as a large, demonic, black dog with flaming eyes and razor sharp teeth.

They are common in British folklore and are known in Wales as the 'Gwyligi', or 'Dog of Darkness and in Cambridgeshire as 'Black Shuck'.

One of these fearful creatures was said to haunt the ravine known as Trollers Gill near Appletreewick in the Yorkshire Dales. It shared its sinister territory with Scandinavian trolls, who were equally as nasty and would hurl rocks at unwary travellers.

Although its name and even its form appear to vary, one detail that the Barguest appears to have in common across Britain is the omen of disaster. In Jersey the 'Tchico' is a warning of an impending storm and, as with other spectral manifestations of the hellhound, it is considered a portent of death.

It's name is thought to derive from the pronunciation of the word ghost as 'guest' by the people of the north of England and the word 'burh', an Anglo-Saxon name for a town or fortress, hence 'burh-guest', or 'town-ghost'. Others think

it may have a German origin in 'Berg-geist, or 'mountain demon' or possibly 'Bar-geist', meaning 'bear demon', as a result of its appearance at times as a bear.

The York Barguest is said to haunt the many alleyways and snickets that tunnel throughout the city and was also reported to have been seen by a guard at the gate of Clifford's Tower on the night of 7th March 1686 following the hanging of a local witch. Investigating a loud noise in the vicinity of the castle porch the guard was witness to a scroll appearing beneath the gate and transforming into a monkey.

After a short while it transformed again into a turkey and, after summoning the under-keeper, both men watched as the apparition returned to its original form of a scroll and disappeared back under the gate.

said to haunt the many alleyways that tunnel throughout the city

02

In the heart of York lies an oasis of tranquility that exudes a peace and calm that belies it's turbulent historical connections. With York Minster towering behind it, two very different apparitions are said to haunt this 15th century church.

the church of HOLY TRINITY

The first, Sir Thomas Percy, the 7th Earl of Northumberland and lover of Anne Boleyn before her marriage to Henry VIII, was beheaded for treason.

Like his namesake father before him, who was executed at Tyburn for his part in the uprising against Henry VIII following the dissolution of some of the smaller monasteries, Sir Thomas conspired against Queen Elizabeth, with the intention of freeing the imprisoned Mary Queen of Scots and re-establishing the Catholic religion that was being eroded by the Protestant monarchy. However, their plot was exposed to the Queen which prompted the leaders to assemble their forces at Durham where they headed south via Staindrop, Darlington, Richmond, and Ripon, restoring the ancient service in each place. At Ripon they defeated the forces of Sir William Ingleby and marched on to Knaresborough, Wetherby, Clifford Moor and their final victory at Barnard Castle. Their next destination was York.

Unfortunately, a 5,000 strong defence was waiting for them. The uprising dissipated and the leaders fled to Scotland. Thomas was betrayed by the Earl of Moreton, Viceroy of Scotland and was taken to York and beheaded in Pavement, his head being stuck on a spike and displayed at Micklegate Bar. Eventually it was buried in the graveyard at Holy Trinity and the Earl's headless torso has been witnessed on many occasions wandering around the grave stones in an endless quest to be re united with his lost head.

the Earls headless torso has been witnessed on many occasions

A plaque affixed to the wall almost directly opposite the entrance to the snicket 'Lady Peckett's Yard' marks the sight of the execution.

The second visitation, which was documented by a clergyman, the Reverend S. Baring Gould in his book 'Yorkshire Oddities' is of a young mother, her face obscured by a veil, who would often appear during daylight hours.

She would then be joined by a second female, described as a nursemaid, who would be accompanied by a small child. The spectres' origin was said to be that of an ill-fated family that lived close to the church. The father died and was buried in the churchyard close to the east window.

Not long after, the child fell victim to the plague which, due to plague regulations, resulted in him being buried outside the city walls. Grief stricken with loss the mother also died relatively soon after and was buried with her husband in the church grounds. The ghostly re-enactment was the mother's continued attempt to re-unite herself with her lost child.

It appears that the re-building of the chancel in 1886 ended the sightings and no further reports have been made since the 1890's.

03

The Yorkshire Museum

Like Holy Trinity Church, the Yorkshire Museum's setting is not initially, suggestive of any dark, unnatural events. Set in ten acres of beautiful botanical gardens the site is also home to the remains of St. Mary's Abbey, a 14th century Hospitium and part of a Roman fortress wall.

However, George Thomas, the caretaker of the museum at the time, suffered an early evening encounter that certainly left him with no doubt that there are 'more things in heaven and Earth...

The year was 1950 when the otherwise unremarkable Mr. Thomas noticed a man dressed in a frock coat reading a book in the museum library. He assumed that the gentleman was a visitor that had become so engrossed in his research that he was unaware of the fact that it was closing time. As he approached the man he realised that he was very agitated and was muttering "I must find it". At this point the figure vanished, dropping the book to the floor.

Having mentioned the incident to a few others a small group gathered one night in the hope that the spectre would re-appear. Although they were to be disappointed by a lack of manifestation they were rewarded by the startling display of a book flying from its shelf and hurtling to the floor with a loud thud. There was also a noticeable drop in the temperature at around the time of this occurrence, something that was in keeping with previous reports of 'an intense cold' by members of the museum staff.

At this point the figure vanished dropping the book to the floor

Having recovered themselves the book was examined and found to be the very same book that had fallen from the hands of the disappearing spook witnessed by George Thomas. The book, 'Antiquities and Curiosities of the Church' had been donated to the museum by Alderman Edward Wooler, a photograph of whom was shown to Mr.Thomas who identified it as the ghost he had seen in the library.

Despite there being no more reported sightings of Alderman Wooler the book was seen to remove itself from shelves and drop to the floor on a number of further occasions by staff at the museum and, although it is not known what he was so anxiously trying to locate, there is a brown stain on the inside cover that may once have had a photograph or document attached to it.

The book was subsequently moved to the City Library where it seemed to be much more settled and all gravity defying acts came to an end. Perhaps, like so many ghosts who seem to be confined to a particular building or place, Alderman Wooler is unable to leave the Yorkshire Museum, in which case, having been separated from the book, he is doomed never to find the item that he was so desperately searching for.

04

The Treasurer's House

In the shadow of York Minster sits a building as important for its history as it is notorious for its ghosts.

Built on a Roman site and originally the mediaeval home of the Minster's treasurer, the house was all but destroyed by the great fire of York in 1137. Rebuilt during the reign of Edward I and substantially altered by Thomas Young during the 1600's, it was bought by the prospering George Aislaby from Lord Fairfax in 1663. By the time the fateful night of January 10th 1647 came about, George Aislaby and his wife were established enough to be invited, along with Mrs. Aislaby's sister Mary Mallorie, to the Duke of Buckingham's ball in Skeldergate. At the party, Mary Mallorie met up with her fiancé, Jonathon Jennings, and failed to return to The Treasurers House later that night. The family's honour clearly impeached, George Aislaby challenged Jennings to a duel at which he was mortally wounded. Buried nearby, his supernatural presence is particularly strong around the Chapterhouse Street entrance.

the soldiers were not visible below their knees

However, the most intriguing and certainly the best known apparitions are the Roman soldiers that appear in the cellar. A young apprentice plumber by the name of Harry Martindale created intense interest when he made some notable observations about the ghosts that were at odds with most people's pre-conceived ideas about Romans. Working in the cellar in the early fifties, Harry's encounter began with the sound of a trumpet blast, followed by the appearance of a Roman on horseback and a procession of foot soldiers. Unlike the shining and disciplined soldiers of Hollywood movies, these men

were dirty and unkempt with a weary look that suggested they had returned from a long journey. Although frightened and unsure of the nature of his experience, Harry was able to take in a number of details that imbued his testimony with a great deal of verity. The poor quality of their clothing, the cross-gartering of their sandals, round shields and the green kilted skirts they were wearing were all features that, although known to be historically correct, were not familiar to people outside academic circles.

In addition, Harry noticed that the soldiers were not visible below their knees. That is, until they reached a section of the cellar where the original Roman road, lying eighteen inches below the cellar floor, had been recently excavated. With no apparent awareness of the presence of the young man watching in amazement at their passing, the Romans vanished into the wall at the opposite side of the cellar.

05

There are a number of 'Grey Ladies' haunting the more spooky parts of York (notably The York Arms and The Starr Inn public houses) but perhaps the most often seen is the hooded figure that portents a successful show at the Theatre Royal.

York Theatre Royal

Founded in 1744 the theatre was built on the ruins of St Leonard's Hospital, the largest medieval hospital in Europe during the 12th century. Parts of the old crypt can still be seen in the Keregan Room and, even older, are the remains of a Roman well beneath the stage. The sad lady that has so often been seen by performers was believed to have been a young apprentice nun working in the hospice. Having committed the dreadful sin of falling in love with a nobleman she was punished by being bricked up alive in a small room adjacent to the dress circle. Subsequently used as a dressing room, her presence has often been felt by the occupants, who have described a feeling of being watched and also a cold, lingering atmosphere.

However, a recent investigation by a group of psychic researchers uncovered some very different information, including the woman's name.

Although it was confirmed that the lady was a nun, the reason for her internment, which was a cell not a brick wall, was for claiming to have seen angels at mass. Accused of possessing a "black and lying tongue", 'Therese' was threatened with harsher punishment if she didn't stay put. Despite the many alterations that have been made to the building over the years, no body has ever been found, which would suggest that the story of Therese is perhaps more accurate.

A second ghost, that of an actor, has been seen on occasion and was first witnessed on the day of his death, apparently as a result of a duel in Blake Street. The rest of the cast decided that, despite the tragedy, the show must go on and were horrified to see their former leading man stumbling around in the wings during the evening's performance.

Seemingly unrelated to either the Grey Lady or the duelling actor is the report in the 1930's of organ music being played in the theatre in the middle of the night. First heard at twenty past two it was repeated an hour later and was never heard again.

her presence has often been felt by the occupants

With the Minster towering above it to the left, the 15th century timber building of St William's College to the right and the Treasurers House just round the corner, number 5 college street is situated in the most densely haunted area in the whole of the city.

College Street

As if that wasn't enough, the house itself dates back to mediaeval times and what is surprising is not that it is haunted but that there is only one ghost. The ghost in question owes its existence to a sad and somewhat harrowing tale of a young girl who died of starvation during the Great Plague of 1604, a plague which killed 3,512 people in a city whose population was only about 10,000.

The details of her story emerged following a requested seance by a family occupying the house in the early part of the twentieth century. People over the years had often complained of an intense sadness that pervades the house, but the two children living there at this time were troubled by a continual crying, footsteps running around the upstairs part of the house and the materialisation, also seen by the nanny, of a young girl in an old fashioned white dress.

The seance revealed that the girl's parents had both died of the plague. The servants mistakenly believed that their daughter, also stricken with the illness, had died along with them and left the property to be boarded up, in line with plague regulations that were designed to isolate infected areas. However, the girl recovered and awoke to find herself abandoned with her dead parents. Small wonder that her ghostly presence should manifest itself as agitated footprints and the sobbing of a lonely, helpless child.

the seance revealed that the girls parents had both died of the plague

07

York Minster

Towering above the centre of York is the largest gothic cathedral in northern Europe. Started in 1220 on the site of the Roman Fortress headquarters by Archbishop Walter de Grey the Minster took over 250 years to complete and is the site of one of the most intriguing of York's ghost stories.

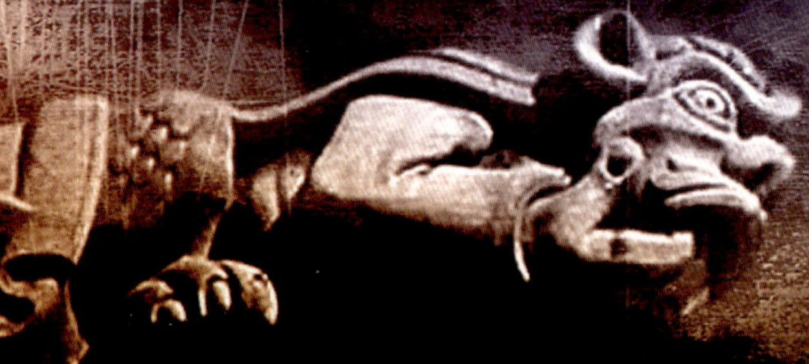

It was recorded in a book published in the middle part of the nineteenth century that a father and his two daughters, whose names were changed to protect the privacy of the family, were being accompanied by a gentleman and a number of other friends on a trip to the Minster. During the course of admiring the vast interior of the building, the gentleman was rather taken aback when a man in naval uniform came walking towards them. As York is some distance from the sea this was an unusual site and he drew the attention of the elder daughter to the fast approaching naval officer. Instead of mild curiosity, the woman appeared intently distressed by the site of the man and she visibly paled. The gentleman called over to the younger daughter and father for some assistance, but by this time the sailor was stood directly in front of them. He leaned over to the woman and whispered a most perplexing statement: "There is a future state", before moving off down the aisle.

Leaving the woman in the care of her father and sister the gentleman went after the man who had caused her such distress but could see nor hear any sign of him. Upon his return the daughter assured her father and sister that she would be fine and that they should leave her in the charge of the gentleman. When they had moved away she explained that the man they had seen was her brother and that she knew that he must have died at sea. She had no wish for her father to know such distressing news and anyway she felt sure

There is a future state

that she would not be believed if she told him. She went on to explain that many years before, she and her brother had made an agreement that whichever one of them died first should, if possible, contact the other at the moment of death.

In time, her story was borne out by the arrival of the news of her brother's death at sea, the date and time coinciding exactly with their encounter in the Minster.

A further apparition in the shape of a monk was witnessed by a Scottish visitor during the York Festival. He was disturbed by the fact that the monk was walking up and down the aisle during the musical performance, but even more disturbed when he discovered that no one else had seen or heard anything.

08

Clifford's Tower

The sight of one York's bloodiest and most shameful episodes, the tower that sits atop the conical motte is the remains of York Castle, built in 1270 to replace the wooden castle that was destroyed by fire. It is known as Clifford's Tower following the execution of Roger de Clifford, who was hung in chains from the walls in 1322 for treason against Edward II.

The original castle was built by William the Conqueror in 1068 but was burnt during an uprising the following year. Its replacement was also burnt following a horrifying event that resulted in the massacre of 150 Jews inside the castle and the death of almost fifteen hundred people during anti-Semitic riots in 1190.

Two leaders of York's Jewish community, Benedict and Jocencus, had travelled to London for the coronation of King Richard but were attacked upon their return to such an extent that Benedict died of his injuries. His house was looted and his wife and children murdered. Jocencus and a large group of his fellow citizens were given permission by the Constable of York Castle to take refuge within the castle but a large mob, incited by the cries of a monk dressed in white, attacked the walls and a number of the trapped Jews committed suicide rather than be taken by the large Christian horde. The survivors opened the doors and begged for mercy, offering large amount s of money for their lives. They were ignored and the rioters murdered every one of them and set the castle ablaze.

the walls of the tower were often observed to turn red

In the years following the massacre the walls of the Tower were often observed to turn red and the phenomenon became known as 'Jew's Blood'. The York Barguest was seen at the gate of the tower in 1686 and, less alarming but much more recently, a members of an overnight ghostwatch in 2005 observed a ghostly Red Setter in the same place.

Bedern

One of the more harrowing tales behind York's catalogue of ghostly sightings takes place around the small street of bedern off Goodramgate

Meaning 'House of Prayer' Bedern was once a square and the home to the College of the Minister's Vicars Choral. The college refectory, or dining hall, is still standing and is currently hired out for private functions (sadly, the bridge which used to link the hall with Minster Close no longer exists). When the Vicars moved out of the square in 1574 the area slowly degenerated and by the end of the eighteenth century a predominantly Irish population were surviving in what was described as a 'sad spectacle of poverty and wretchedness'.

Within this area stood a house that had been used as an old people's home since 1575. In 1847 the residents were moved out and the building became the York Industrial Ragged School, whose master was tasked with the responsibility of rounding up the homeless children of York and, under his care, setting them to work. It became apparent that the man was more interested in the level of his income than the welfare of the children and money that was intended for food and clothing for those in his charge was kept for himself, with the result that many of the children died of starvation or exposure. During warmer weather he would bury the dead in shallow graves but in winter, when the ground became too hard to dig, he would hide the bodies in a large cupboard and leave them to rot. In time, the mounting bodies and increased consumption of alcohol resulted in him hearing screams from the padlocked cupboard and before long his wretched state drove him to murder the remaining living children with a knife. He was arrested and committed to an asylum where he lived out the remainder of his life.

Bedern has been extensively developed over the years since then but the ghostly sound of children playing is still being reported, with the chilling addition that if one stops to listen, the playful noise soon becomes the sound of children screaming.

the ghostly sound of children playing is still being reported

10

Named after St William of York, the nephew of King Stephen, St William's College is a beautiful timbered building sitting in the shadow of the east front of York Minster. Built in 1461 it was originally the home of the Minster's Chantry Priests, but in the first half of the seventeenth century it housed the printing presses of King Charles I during England, Scotland and Ireland's first civil war.

St William's College

The resident ghost is thought to date from the time of the clergy's occupation of the building when it is reputed that two brothers who lived among the upper rooms had murdered a fellow priest. In an act of self preservation the eldest brother had informed the authorities and told them that they would find his sibling hiding in an oak closet within one of the rooms. Unable to face his brother on returning to the college, he paced the corridors of the building in an agitated state of guilt and regret. The authorities finally showed and duly removed the informed upon brother from his hiding place and later hanged him for the crime. The elder brother, having given evidence against him, was spared the same fate. However, a worse fate awaited him as his guilt and remorse were such that his soul became condemned to pace the corridors of the college in an eternal sate of distress.

An additional story, chronicled in The Wortlebank Diary by Holme Lee published in 1860, became associated with the building's later use when it was converted into rented apartments. An engraver by the name of Nicholas Drew rented a complete floor in the upper part of the college. During a particularly cold and snowy New Year's Eve, Nicholas found a young girl crying in the courtyard porch of the college. A fellow tenant identified the child as belonging to a woodcarver who also lived within the college building. On discovering the father dead, Nicholas resolved to keep the child and raise her as his own. Many years later, the child now a woman, Nicholas and his adopted daughter argued over the attentions being paid to her by a humourless character by the name of Laurence Royston. On forbidding her to see him, Royston paid Nicholas a visit and an angry confrontation led to Nicholas being murdered. Next to the bloody body of the man he had just killed, Royston noticed a large oak cabinet, a cabinet that had allegedly belonged to the two brothers who had murdered the priest.

Deciding to make the death look like the work of thieves, he broke into the cabinet and pulled out its contents. Moving back into the main room of the apartment, Royston was confronted by the sound of heavy footsteps, slow and unmistakable, moving towards him. However, besides himself and the dead Nicholas, the room was completely empty.

... his guilt and remorse were such that his soul became condemned to pace the corridors of the college in an eternal sate of distress

11

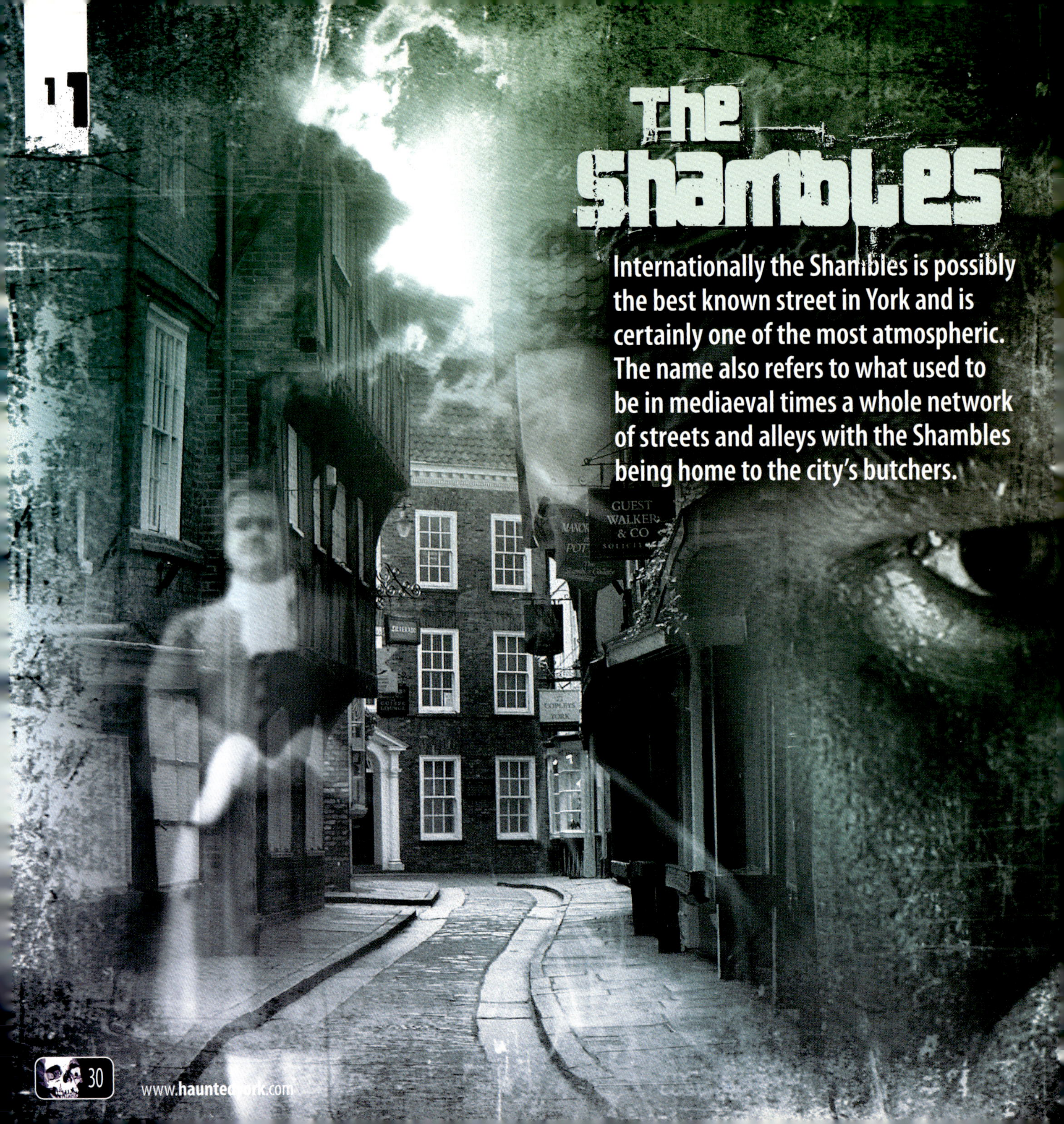

The Shambles

Internationally the Shambles is possibly the best known street in York and is certainly one of the most atmospheric. The name also refers to what used to be in mediaeval times a whole network of streets and alleys with the Shambles being home to the city's butchers.

Many of the buildings that lined these streets and formed the walls of the alleyways are long gone, as are all the butchers, but the Shambles is still very much alive and well, hosting primarily tourist themed shops, but still proudly displaying it's heritage, with many of the shops still sporting the Shamels, or benches, that gave the street it's name.

At the top of the street, on the corner of Pavement, is the site of the St. Crux (Holy Cross) church. Having fallen into disrepair and become unsafe, the church was demolished in 1886, but not before a number of spectres had become associated with the building. A number of people saw a man standing within the church and looking out at the street. As he tended to appear very early in the morning and never made any attempt to come out of the church (and no one dared go in) it was assumed he was a ghost. In addition to this gentleman was a lady, apparently dressed in white, who would follow the York Waits, a group of watchmen whose duties also included the provision of music for the general populace and would do so by roaming the streets kitted out in colourful attire and silver badges. The lady in white would emerge, somewhat alarmingly, from the St Crux churchyard and follow at a respectful distance, clearly enjoying the music, but would not answer to any of the calls made to her by the musicians. She would remain with them until they entered Goodramgate, at which point she would vanish.

A third haunting was experienced by a policeman in the early part of the twentieth century, when his rounds took him late one night past the front of the church. As he walked towards the Shambles he was struck by the eerie sound of a funeral march emanating from within the church, which was clearly strange considering the lateness of the hour. As he stood and listened, the doors of the church swung open and the noise of a procession joined that of the organ music. Although he could see no one, he felt the brush of their clothes against his legs as they passed by. Once the noise of their movement had died away, the church doors swung shut and all became silent.

The lady in white would emerge somewhat alarmingly from the St Crux churchyard

12

The King's Manor

Of all the haunted sites in York the King's Manor seems to have the highest spectral activity of any of the ancient buildings in "Europe's most haunted city". For a building that has been so involved in York's history it seems fitting that it seems to have carefully collected ghostly relics of some of its most notable inhabitants.

Built around 1270 to serve as the Abbot's Residence of St Mary's Abbey, its most veteran occupant is a black hooded monk who has been sighted in various places around the Manor. The remains of the Abbey, to the rear of the King's Manor, are sited in what is now the Museum Gardens. With the abolition of the monasteries by Henry VIII in 1536, the Manor became the seat of the Council of the North and subsequently the official residence of the President of the Council in 1561. The Earl of Huntingdon, who was President between 1572 and 1595, oversaw a great deal of building and extension work that included dressed stonework blocks, known as ashlar, using stone from St Mary's Abbey. Perhaps our hooded monk is keeping an eye on it.

Continued ...

> **The wailing of the dying following the unsuccessful attempt to take the manor on Trinity Sunday in 1644 can still be heard**

Keeping him company is the ghost of Queen Catherine Howard, who, along with her husband Henry VIII, were guests at the manor in 1541. Catherine was only eighteen when the fifty year old Henry took her as his fifth wife and it is perhaps not surprising that very soon after the wedding she entered into affairs with two much younger men. One of these, Thomas Culpepper, indulged in clandestine meetings with the Queen during her stay at the Manor and perhaps it was this happy, although fatally dangerous period that keeps her spectral presence in residence. An interesting detail of her sighting, most notably by a maid who was greeted by the sight of the Queen attired in a flowing green Tudor dress and walking at her through a cupboard, is that she appeared to be carrying what at first were thought to be ribbons. After a number of further sightings by the maid, she realised that they were not ribbons but a bunch of roses. Catherine was sometimes known by the King's reference to her as "the rose without a thorn" and it was later discovered by folklorist John Mitchell that a rose garden had once existed in the opposite direction to the route of the ghost. Shortly after her stay at the Manor, her adultery was discovered and her young lover was hung, drawn and quartered. She herself was arrested and taken to the Tower of London by barge, where she was forced to endure the spectacle of her two lover's heads sitting atop spikes above Tower Bridge. Within a few weeks she was beheaded on Tower Green for treason.

As if by way of solidarity there is the ghost of Thomas Wentworth, President of the Council and Earl of Stafford, who also fell foul of an angry King when Charles I signed his death warrant by consenting to a Bill of Attainder. Once part of English common law, the bill effectively gave the right of the King or Queen to find somebody guilty, usually of treason, without a trial. Like the Queen before him, Thomas was removed to the Tower in 1641 and subsequently beheaded. He was witnessed by an employee of the Manor who recognised him from a portrait that hung in the same room. The incident so disturbed the man that he died later that night.

Within just a few years of the untimely dispatch of Thomas Wentworth, the King's Manor was able to add to its collection of spectral residents when it was besieged by Roundheads during the English civil War. The wailing of the dying following the unsuccessful attempt to take the Manor on Trinity Sunday in 1644 can still be heard emanating from the passage leading away from the inner courtyard.

With the advent of the Stuart Dynasty in 1603, Britain became a United Kingdom and the Manor played its part in a flourishing Court culture, that saw regular visits from the royalty throughout the period and a new building added to the Manor's existing layout. A modest period of poltergeist activity was witnessed by a teacher staying at the Manor, during the years when it was home to the Yorkshire School for the Blind from 1833 until 1956. A cupboard set into the wall would be mysteriously opened as if by some unseen hand but, oddly, this only happened on occasions when she hung a particular scarf within it, a scarf of Royal Stuart Tartan.

A further Stuart connection comes from reports of a Stuart nobleman being seen and the subsequent witness by four teachers who were determined to verify his existence one Halloween. They saw the lower half of the body as the ghost descended the stairs, regaled in appropriate Stuart period attire, but were foiled in their attempt to see more when the headmaster of the school appeared and told them all to go to bed, at which point the ghost vanished.

They saw the lower half of the body as the ghost descended the stairs regaled in appropriate Stuart period attire

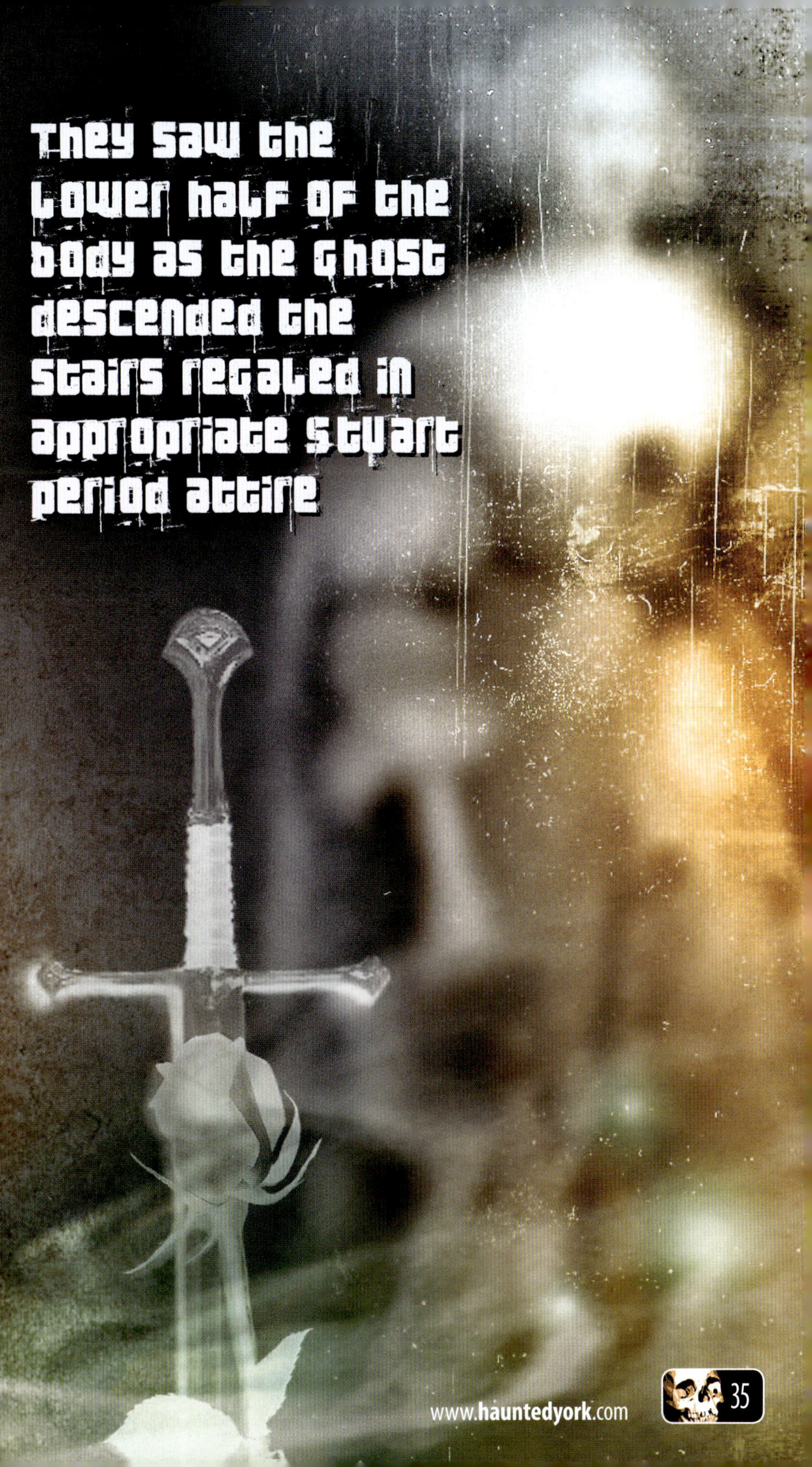

CASTLE MUSEUM

York Castle Museum

Housed in the former York Castle's debtor's and female prisons and sitting in the shadow of the Eye of York, the Castle Museum experiences ghostly disturbances that are being reported even to this day. In addition to the large amount of history on display, including a mock up of a Victorian Street with period costumed actors and authentic sounds, the original use of the buildings adds an historic weight and atmosphere that may account for a good many of the spectral experiences.

It's most famous inmate was the highwayman Dick Turpin, who, despite the glorification of William Harrison Ainsworth's 1834 novel 'Rookwood', was a vicious thief who fled his home county of Essex after shooting dead a gamekeeper, who was attempting to capture Turpin for the fifty pounds reward money. Having adopted the name John Palmer, he established what appears to have been a successful business as a horse trader but his success came largely as a result of supplementing his stock by stealing. This fact came to light when he shot a rooster that belonged to the landlord of the Ferry Inn in Brough in East Yorkshire.
The subsequent investigation resulted in Turpin spending the last six months of his life in the castle prison, before being executed at Tyburn on York's Knavesmire in 1739. Weird scratching, disembodied voices and the rattling of chains have all been heard by museum staff emanating from the cells.

There have also been a number of reports by visitors of an old woman dressed in black, sitting by a fireplace, and also of singing. A man dressed in black has also been witnessed, and may be the ghost of a vicar, and there have also been sightings of a spectral dog.

> Weird scratching disembodied voices and the rattling of chains have all been heard

14

In addition to the apparently vast number of ghosts in York, there are is an equally large number of public houses. By no means mutually exclusive, one fact may go a long way toward accounting for the other, hence our round up of the most prominent haunted taverns in the city centre.

the Haunted Pubs of York

Slightly off the more commonly beaten track to the south of the river is **The Cock and Bottle**, whose resident spook is thought to be that of the seventeenth century nobleman George Villiers, the second Duke of Buckingham. Villiers was a close childhood friend of King Charles II but seemed to spend most of his life engaging in behaviour designed to annoy and embarrass him, including indulging in an affair with the Countess of Shrewsbury and subsequently shooting her husband in a duel. Amongst his many skills and interests was the art and science of alchemy. He told the theologian Thomas Burnet that he was very close to finding the philosophers stone, a substance that could transmute base metal into gold and provide the elixir of life. It is thought that he had a laboratory on or near the site of the Cock and Bottle and may have spent a good portion of the time following his retirement from Parliament in the quest for regaining his youth. Although his apparition is not particularly well formed he has been seen on a number of occasions, dressed in suitably refined clothing, but only by women. A former landlady saw him when she was taking a shower and other young woman have reported being stroked or fondled. He has also been seen sitting by the fire. There have also been sightings of 'an ugly man' which may not be Villiers as he was known to be attractive. There have also been reports of ghostly noises, including the sound of a breaking door.

Coming into the city over Ouse Bridge and following High Ousegate into Pavement you'll find **The Golden Fleece**, York's 'most haunted pub'. It is also a pub of considerable pedigree, with a reference to the building in the York archives as far back as 1503, when it was owned by The Merchant Adventurers. It was their capacity as woollen traders that resulted in the name of the pub, which was licensed as far back as 1668 and became a popular coaching inn during the early part of the eighteenth century, when it was under the ownership of John Peckitt, the Lord Mayor of York. The Mayor's wife, Lady Alice Peckett, gave her name to the yard at the rear of the pub and, the street that accesses the yard is now also known by her name. Her ghost has been seen on a number of occasions, usually in the early hours of the morning, and shares the labyrinthine corridors with a woman attired in a Victorian dress, who vanishes through the wall into the shop next door. A Canadian airman who came to a violent end when he fell from an upstairs room has been witnessed and a number of people claim that they have felt a small boy pulling at their legs when they've been sat down. It may not be the only leg pulling going on, but someone claimed to have seen the ghost of 'One Eyed Jack', dressed in sixteenth or seventeenth century costume and there has also been a report of a woman dressed in black in the St Catherine's Room.

Leaving the Golden Fleece you will find yourself opposite the entrance to York's most famous street, The Shambles (haunted place No. 11 in our book). Little remains of the network of alleyways that once occupied this area in the days when

PUNCH
BOWL
Fleece
The haunted
pubs of old York

it was populated by the city's butcher industry, but near the top is Little Shambles, which leads into the modern market square and Silver Street. Emerging from the busy market will find you facing St. Sampson's Square, in the corner of which is the **Roman Bath**, a pub that is as keen on live music as it is on the archaeological heritage that gives it its name. Unsurprisingly considering the seventeen hundred year time span since their occupation, there is very little remaining of the Roman presence. However, for a small fee you can go below the Roman Bath inn and stand amid the remains of a caldarium, or steam bath and also the remains of a neighbouring plunge bath.

These were discovered in 1930 during renovation work and there is also a small museum with Roman related exhibits. Various ghostly experiences have been reported by visitors including the sound of footsteps and also the sound of splashing water. A decorator painting the walls at the foot of the staircase that leads into the baths refused to continue, claiming that "something was there" and a couple in 2006 reported feeling a presence and capturing a strange light anomaly on their mobile phone camera. Perhaps the most extraordinary experience was that of a previous landlord and his friend who, in the early 1990's, took it upon themselves to stay the night in the baths as a means of raising money for charity and also raising awareness of the pub and its ancient remains. As the men were settling down for the night ahead they both witnessed the same thing: an extremely bright light that was accompanied by the figure of a person. The manifestation did not last long and appeared to fade out into the area occupied by the excavated 'cold-room', although one of the men witnessed the light again a fortnight later. The cynics amongst you may be wondering whether the whole thing was made up by the landlord as a publicity stunt, in which case it's worth pointing out that following this incident he resigned.

... Ghostly footsteps have also been heard on the floor boards above people's heads

Turning right as you exit the Roman Bath takes you up Finkle Street and into Swinegate, Little Stonegate and ultimately Stonegate itself. One of the main shopping streets in York, Stonegate boasts two haunted pubs, the first of which is **The Punchbowl**. Low beamed ceilings and dark wood panelling certainly create a suitably atmospheric environment and there are at least three ghosts said to inhabit the old rooms and cellar. A former landlord who died in a fire has been heard descending the cellar steps and a strange, disembodied glowing head has been seen floating just above the floor of the back room. Below this back room is the cellar, which at some point was lowered from six feet to five, suggesting that it is either the head of the landlord, continuing on after reaching the foot of the stairs, with the remainder of his ghostly body hidden beneath the floor, or it is the apparition of a six foot tall man who apparently died in the cellar shortly before the ceiling was lowered. Somewhat more frantic ghostly footsteps have also been heard on the floorboards above people's heads. These are thought to belong to a girl who worked at the pub at a time when it was also acting as a brothel. Having made the fatal error of resisting the attention of a drunken client, he pursued her from room to room, eventually throttling her to death. The sound of her last, desperate minutes, as she attempts to evade her nemesis, seem to be recorded into the very fabric of the building. There is also the ubiquitous 'grey lady', in this case the forlorn spirit of a rejected woman who took her own life. Even death has not brought her peace, as she repeatedly returns in the hope of finding her lost lover.

The desperate cries of the wounded and dying have been heard all round the pub ...

Walking up Stonegate with the ever present Minster ahead, you will notice an advertising banner stretching over the street. Below it to the left is the entrance to the banner's subject, **The Olde Starre Inn**. York's oldest licensed pub, it was built in the sixteenth century but the cellars may date back as far as the tenth. The Civil War brought the pain of the locally fought Battle of Marston Moor in 1644 to the inn, when the Roundheads used it as a billet hospital and morgue, despite the Royalist sympathies and annoyance of the landlord, William Foster. The desperate cries of the wounded and dying have been heard all round the pub and the screams of the makeshift operating theatre still emanate from the ancient cellar. There is also a story concerning two cats that were apparently bricked up alive in the pillar that separates the bar from the door. People have heard them running through the bar and dogs bark and make futile attempts to reach them through the pillar. An old lady has also been witnessed by children climbing the stairs.

Onward to the end of Stonegate and left into Low Petergate will take you towards the West face of the Minster and Bootham Bar. On the

The Snickleway Inn

right, just as you enter High Petergate, is the **York Arms**, a pub that was originally a coffee house. The spirits that visit this pub seem to have wandered out of their proper haunts and gone for a walk. One is a blurry grey lady who is the sad remnant of a nun who was punished for the sin of becoming pregnant by being walled up in a nearby church building. This may be the same figure that a number of witnesses have testified to being a young woman, an old woman and a child. An unknown woman apparently pops up at unexpected moments in the gent's toilets (not that there would ever be expected moments) and became so annoying to one former landlord while he was trying to decorate that he threw a paintbrush at her. It is thought that she may be the same ghost that haunts the Theatre Royale which is close by. There have also been reports of poltergeist activity resulting in objects being moved or even thrown, doors apparently opening and closing or even locking themselves, and ashtrays being tipped over.

Left out of the York Arms and you'll be right in front of the imposing west face of York Minster, which local folklore attests to being the fourth windiest spot in Europe. Running to the right of the Minster is Minster Yard which runs into Deangate, now pedestrianised as a result of concerns that the traffic might cause the old church to fall down. Turning right off Deangate into Goodramgate and you'll see the **Snickleway Inn** on the left, sporting a magnificently eerie pub sign depicting the alleyway that gives the pub its name. The name is actually a different spelling of the word 'Snickelway', which is in itself a made up word by author Mark Jones for a book he published in 1983 that details all the passages and alleyways that snake through the centre of York. Dating back to the late fifteenth century and renovated in the late sixteenth century, the pub boasts a number of ghosts including a four year old girl who was the victim of a tragic accident involving a brewer's dray and a woman by the name of Mrs Tulliver who is kept company by her spectral cat. There is also an old man who has been seen walking through the pub and then dematerialising and an Elizabethan man dressed in a blue doublet who has been seen standing behind the bar. Another example of poltergeist activity occurs within the cellar when barmen have had spanners thrown at them and there have been a number or reports of a strong smell of lavender that permeates

There is also an old man who has been seen walking through the pub and then de-materialising ...

the inn. It has been suggested that the latter is connected to the outbreaks of plague that hit York in 1604 and 1631 when lavender was used to mask the stench of the dead and dying victims. In addition, there is the ghost of Marmaduke Buckle, who has been seen occasionally in one of the first floor rooms, and also seen from the outside of the pub staring down into Goodramgate from the window. Marmaduke actually lived with his wealthy parents next door to the pub at the turn of the eighteenth century, and by all accounts was a deeply unhappy young man. Afflicted with a number of physical handicaps he was shunned and persecuted by his peers and eventually felt so wretched that he saw death as his only escape. Carving his name, the year of his birth and also what was to be the year of his death into the wall plaster, he then hung himself from a wooden beam.

People have reported ghostly voices talking to each other

Continuing up Goodramgate you only have a short walk to **The Old White Swan** on the other side of the road. The pub occupies a space once taken up by nine different buildings that were home to a diverse range of occupants including a barber, a poultry market and a pigsty. By the end of the eighteenth century it had become a major coaching inn with stabling for about thirty horses . A relic from this time in the form of four steps known as 'mountings' can still be seen in the entrance courtyard and were used by passengers for boarding and disembarking from the coaches. The parish records of 1723 make note of the instruction to local constables to be vigilant of the illegal activities of the papists, supporters of the Roman Catholic church that were still being persecuted as a result of the reformation, and who would gather in secret to discuss their recusant beliefs. The Old White Swan is thought to have been one of their meeting places, and staff have reported ghostly occurrences with chairs, that would be found in a circle around the fire which would have mysteriously lit itself. On one occasion chairs were seen flying around in the air before suddenly crashing to the floor and people have reported ghostly voices talking to each other.

If your nerve has not deserted you by this point and assuming you're still capable of walking there is one more tavern on this ghostly tour that it is well worth a visit. Reaching the end of Goodramgate and turning left into Colliergate will take you to the junction of Stonebow. Turn left and walk for a few minutes and **The Black Swan** will come into view on the opposite side of the road. Although built in 1417 it was the mid eighteenth century before it became a pub, during which time there were also structural alterations.

However, it appears not to have changed at all since then, and walking through the solid oak door at the pub's front entrance is a bit like stepping back in time. A regular spectral visitor is a gentleman in a bowler hat who walks around the pub as though expecting to meet somebody but invariably just disappears. There is also a young woman, her face hidden with long, black hair and attired in a suitably gothic white dress who stares vacantly into the fire and the landlord has reported seeing a disembodied pair of male legs walking around his accommodation.

Ghost Walks

A guide to haunted York would not be complete without giving details of the professional story tellers that ply their trade through the cities most ghost infected streets and alleys. Contemporary folklorists, they keep the stories alive and entertain in a manner that is fast becoming a dying art.

The Original Ghost Walk

Promises a unique opportunity to discover the hidden magic of the Ancient City of York through the real art of storytelling. Tales are drawn from the immense History of York and are told against a back drop of haunting beauty. The Original Ghost Walk was established in 1973 and was an original creation believed to be the first in the world. The walk is accurate, authentic and genuine and there are no stage managed tricks or gimmicks, just a fun night out for all. All guides are City, County (Blue Badge) or Equity qualified.

Time:	8pm.
Place:	Departs from the Kings Arms Pub, King's Staith.
Prices:	Adults £4 • Children £2.50.
Dates:	Every night except Christmas Day
Contact:	Mr and Mrs Graham.
Tel:	01759 373 090 or +44 (0) 1904 764 222
E-mail:	ghostwalk.ofyork@talk21.com
Website:	www.yorkshirenet.co.uk/yorkghostwalk

The Ghost Hunt of York

The only Ghost walk to ever win The York Tourism bureau 'City tour of the year'. Whatever the weather and always on time, the Victorian guide with his frock coat, top hat and Gladstone bag manifests himself at the strike of half past seven at the bottom of Shambles, England's most famous mediaeval street. Ringing his death bell he gathers the awaiting ghost hunters and leads on to York`s darker side. The Ghost Hunt never cancels. Always elevated, the guide can be seen and heard by everyone and children are encouraged to come to the front. At each location the guide directs the crowd to optimum positions. The Ghost Hunt presents classic York ghost stories in a captivating style, no tardy tales of tedium but intelligent, energetic accounts from a guide with a predilection for fun and entertainment. "Takes your emotions from Horror to Hilarity".

Time:	7.30pm.
Place:	Departs from the Shambles.
Prices:	Adults £5 • Children £3.
Dates:	Every night.
Contact:	Andy Dextrous.
Tel:	+44 (0) 1904 608 700.
E-mail:	dextrous@ghosthunt.co.uk
Website:	www.ghosthunt.co.uk

The Ghost Trail of York

Dare you travel back in time, cross the centuries and experience the stories that make up the hidden and blood chilling history of York's ghostly tradition? Traditional tales, Victorian tragedies and true accounts of modern day ghostly phenomena: interweave with dark figures that lurk in the shadows to create a spine tingling experience that will haunt you forever. Yorkshire Tourist Board White Rose Awards for Tourism finalist 2006.

Time:	7.30pm prompt.
Place:	Departs from the West doors of York Minster.
Prices:	Adult £4 • Children £2 • Concessions £3.
Dates:	Every night except Christmas Day, Boxing Day and New Years Day.
Contact:	Mr. Greg Preston.
Tel:	+44 (0) 1904 633 276.
Website:	www.ghosttrail.co.uk

Haunted Walk of York

Presenting the world famous Haunted Walk of York. This is a historical ghost walk so no masks or gimmicks, just traditional story telling at it's best. Let the experienced guide tell you of the hauntings, sightings, murders and mysteries behind the most haunted City in Europe. This tour has featured on national TV and Radio. It is also recommended by the best guide books in the world.

Time:	8pm.
Place:	Departs from outside the Art Gallery on Exhibition Square.
Prices:	Adults £4 • Children £2 • Concessions £3.
Dates:	Sunday 12th November to Saturday 10th March: Friday and Saturday. Sunday 25th March to Saturday 10th November: Every night.
Contact:	Mr T. Mercer.
Tel:	+44 (0) 1904 621 003.
E-mail:	thehauntedwalkofyork@hotmail.com

Ghost Cruise – York Boat

Join the 'spirits' at the bar for an entertaining one hour evening cruise with costumed story teller. Light-hearted, fun and suitable for ghost-hunters young and old.

Time:	31st March to 20th July: 7pm (boarding from 6.30pm) 21st July to 2nd September: 7pm (boarding from 6.30pm) and 8.30pm (boarding from 8pm) 3rd September to 31st October: 7pm (boarding from 6.30pm)
Place:	Boarding at King's Staith landing.
Prices:	Adult £9 • Children £5.50 • Seniors £8 • Family £24 (up to 2 adults, 3 children) • Under 5 Free.
Dates:	31st March to 31st October: Every night.
Contact:	YorkBoat, The Boatyard, Lendal Bridge, York, YO1 7DP.
Tel:	+44 (0)1904 628324.
Fax:	+44 (0)1904 647204.
E-mail:	info@yorkboat.co.uk
Website:	www.yorkboat.co.uk

The Ghost Detective

The Ghost Detective does not need tricks or bags full of props to help with his storytelling. Instead, he relies only on his wit, knowledge and skill. Simply dressed in his trademark Homburg hat and black cravat, he will take you to parts of old York that even some long-standing residents never knew existed. Making your way around the dimly-lit streets, you will become aware that the Ghost Detective does not merely tell the traditional ghost stories of York, he actively researches them, along with any new sightings which may occur. With the Ghost Detective, you can rest assured that you have found a dynamic tour with the very latest secrets of the supernatural, delivered in a traditionally British style, with one of the most beautiful cities in the world as its backdrop.

Time:	7.30pm.
Place:	Departs from outside the Jorvik Viking Centre in Coppergate Walk.
Prices:	Adult £4 • Children £2 • Concessions £2.
Dates:	Every night from Easter to Hallowe'en. Every Friday, Saturday and Sunday from November to March.
Contact:	Ghost Detective Tour of York.
Tel:	07947 325 239.
E-mail:	inquiries@ghostdetective.com
Website:	www.ghostdetective.com

To assist you in your York ghost hunting we've compiled the following information on the locations that are public buildings. Please be aware that this information may be subject to change. The number corresponds to the number on the map.

4 Treasurer's House

Address: Minster Yard, York YO1 7JL.

Open: 18th March to 5th November, Saturday to Thursday 11am to 4.30pm.

Admission: House and Garden: Adult £5.00 • Child £2.50 • Family £12.50 (2 adults and 3 children).
Groups of 15 Adult £3.50 • Child £1.70.
House and Cellar: Adult £7.00 • Child £4.00.
Cellar (NT members): Adult £2 • Child £1.50.

Facilities: Tearoom, art gallery, baby changing.

Contact: Telephone : +44 (0) 1904 624247

E-mail: treasurershouse@nationaltrust.org.uk

Website: www.nationaltrust.org.uk

7 York Minster

Address: Deangate, York YO1 7HH

Open: April to October: Monday to Saturday 9.00am to 5.00pm, Sunday 12.00pm to 3.45pm. November to March: 9.30am to 5.00pm, Sunday 12.00pm to 3.45pm.
The Tower: Monday to Saturday 9.30am to 5pm, Sunday 12.30pm to 5pm. (No children under 8 allowed in the Tower).
The Undercroft: Monday to Saturday 9.30am to 5pm, Sunday 12.30pm to 5pm.
Closed Christmas Eve, Christmas Day and Good Friday.

Admission: Adults £5.00 • Concessions £4.00 • Children free of charge.
Undercroft, Treasury and Crypt (includes free audio tour): Adults £4.00 • Children £2.00 • Concessions £3.00.
Minster and Undercroft, Treasury and Crypt combined (includes free audio tour): Adults £7.00 • Concessions £5.00 • Children £2.00. Entry to the Tower: Adults £3.50 • Children £2.00.

Facilities: Shop, toilets, guided tours (when available).

Contact: The Visitors Department :

Telephone: +44 (0) 1904 557 216

E-mail: visitors@yorkminster.org

Website: www.yorkminster.org

information

2 Holy Trinity Church

Address: Off Goodramgate, York YO1 2LF.
Open: April to September: Monday to Saturday 10am–5pm, Sunday 12pm–5pm. October to March: Tuesday to Saturday 10am to 4pm.
Admission: Free of charge.
Facilities: None.
Contact: Telephone : +44 (0) 1904 613 451
E-mail: wetherall.tcct@virgin.net
Website: www.visitchurches.org.uk

5 York Theatre Royal

Address: St Leonard's Place, York YO1 7HD.
Open: Box Office: Monday 10am to 6pm. Tuesday to Saturday 10am to 8pm.
Admission: Performance ticket price.
Facilities: Café (Wi-Fi enabled), bars and restaurant.
Contact: Box Office:
Telephone: +44 (0) 1904 623 568
Fax (01904) 550 164
E-mail: admin@yorktheatreroyal.co.uk
Website: www.yorktheatreroyal.co.uk

8 Clifford's Tower

Address: Tower Street, York, YO1 9SA.
Open: 1st April to 30th September: Daily 10am to 6pm.
October: Daily 10am to 5pm.
1st November to 31st March: Daily 10am until 4pm.
Admission: Adults £3.00 • Children (under 16) £1.30 • Concessions £2.30 • Family tickets (2+3) £7.50.
Facilities: Gift shop. Braille panels and booklet.
Contact: Telephone : +44 (0) 1904) 646 940

10 St William's College

Address: 4-5 College St, York YO1 7JF.
Open: Halls: Daily 9am to 5pm.
Cafe: Daytime 10am to 5pm, evening 6.30pm to 9.30pm.
Restaurant: Sunday to Monday 10.30am to 5pm.
Tuesday to Saturday 10.30am to 10pm.
Admission: Adults £1 • Children 50p.
Facilities: Tearoom, cafe, restaurant, exhibition, conference and function rooms. Licensed for alcohol.
Contact: Phone: +44 (0)1904 634 830

information

3 Yorkshire Museum

Address: Museum Street, York Y01 7FR.

Open: Daily from 10am to 5pm
Closed 25th and 26th December and 1st January.

Gardens: 12th February to 25th February: 7.30am to 6pm.
26th February to 11th March: 7.30am to 6.30pm.
12th March to 25th March: 7.30am to 7pm.
From 26th March: 7.30am to 8pm.

Admission: Tickets are valid for a whole year: Adult £5 • Child £3.50 • Under 5 Free • Concessions £4. Residents with a York Card Free. Two adults with: One child £12 • Two children £15 and £3 per child after that.
Joint tickets for entry to Yorkshire Museum and York Castle Museum: Adult £9 • Child £5 • Under 5 free • Concessions £7.50. Two adults with: One child £21.50 • Two children £26 and £4.50 per child after that.

Facilities: Gift shop.

Contact: Telephone : +44 (0) 1904 687 687

E-mail: info@yorkshiremuseum.org.uk

Website: www.yorkshiremuseum.org.uk

13 York Castle Museum

Address: Castle Area, Eye of York, York, Y01 9RY.

Open: 9.30am to 5pm.
Closed 25th and 26th December and 1st January.
Open 10am on Fridays during school term times.

Admission: Tickets are valid for a whole year: Adult £6.50 • Child £3.50 • Under 5's Free • Concessions £5.
Residents with a York Card Free.
Wheelchair users plus one carer Free.
Two adults with: One child £15 • Two children £18 and £3 per child after that.
Joint tickets for entry to York Castle Museum and the Yorkshire Museum: Adult £9 • Child £5 • Under 5's Free • Concessions £7.50.
Two adults with: One child £21.50 • Two children £26 and £4.50 per child after that.

Facilities: Cafe open between 10am and 4pm.

Contact: Phone: +44 (0) 1904 650 333
Fax: +44 (0) 1904 671 078

Website: www.yorkcastlemuseum.co.uk

12 The King's Manor

Address: Exhibition Square, University of York, York, YO1 2EP.
Open: Monday to Thursday 10am to 4pm, Friday 10am to 3:45pm
Admission: Free.
Facilities: Tearoom, Restaurant. Licensed for alcohol.
Contact: Phone: +44 (0) 1904 43 3995
Fax: +44 (0) 1904 43 3996

York Ghost Festival

The first of York's annual Ghost Festivals was in 2003 and included a public ghost vigil at the Golden Fleece pub. Among a variety of reported spookiness was the apparition of a fully formed gentleman who appeared through one wall, walked across a corridor and vanished through the opposite wall. Organised by PSI (Paranormal and Spectral Investigations) this year's festival runs from Friday, October 26th to Wednesday, October 31st 2007.

If you're brave enough to be involved in the fun, visit www.yorkghostfestival.co.uk for more information.

E-mail: ghostfinder.general@gmail.com
Website: www.yorkghostfestival.co.uk

Ghost Photographs

The ideal way to commemorate your ghostly visit to York is to become a ghost. While you're exploring The Shambles (page 30) have a look in Past Images, who will cheerfully cause your death and spectral resurrection by the wonder of digital photography. As they are also a period costume photographic studio you can also dress up as an ancient resident of the city before having your head chopped off.

Address: 10 Shambles, York YO1 7LZ.
Open: Open seven days a week.
Winter Opening:
Sunday 11am-5pm,
Saturday 10am-5pm,
Monday-Friday 11am-3pm.
Summer Opening:
Sunday 10am-5pm,
Saturday 10am-5pm,
Monday-Friday 10am-5pm.
Contact: Phone: +44 (0) 1904 676 167.
E-mail: info@pastimages.co.uk
Website: www.past-images.co.uk

City of York
Gillygate
Bootham
Bootham Bar
Precentor's Ct.
High Petergate
St. Leonard's Pl
Duncome Pl
Minster Yard
Minster Gates
Deangate
Chapter Ho
College Street
Goodramgate
Bedern
Bartle
Low Petergate
Stonegate
Grape La
Little Stonegate
Back Swinegate
Swinegate
Finkle St.
Church Street
King's Ct.
Patrick Pool
Newgate
King's Sq
Blake Street
Museum Street
Lendal
Davygate
St. Helen's Sq
New St.
St. Sampson's Sq
Silver St.
Jubbergate
Little Shambles
Parliament
Feasegate
Market Street
Lendal Bridge
River Ouse
Coney Street
Spurriergate
High Ousegate
Ness Gt.
Ousegate
Ouse Bridge
Bridge Street
Skeldergate
King Street
King's Staith
Cumberland
N
NE
E
SE
1
2
3
4
5
6
7
8
9
10
12

HAUNTED PLACES

1. The York Barguest
2. The Church of Holy Trinity
3. The Yorkshire Museum
4. The Treasurer's House
5. York Theatre Royal
6. College Street
7. York Minster
8. Clifford's Tower
9. Bedern
10. St William's College
11. The Shambles
12. The King's Manor
13. The Castle Museum

HAUNTED PUBS

1. The Golden Fleece
2. The Punchbowl Stonegate
3. The Cock & Bottle, Skeldergate
4. The Old White Swan, Goodramgate
5. The York Arms, Low Petergate
6. The Olde Starre Inn, Stonegate
7. The Black Swan – Peaseholme Green
8. The Snickleway Inn – 47 Goodramgate
9. The Roman Bath – St Sampson's Square
10. Dean Court Hotel – Duncombe Place

EPILOGUE

We hope you've enjoyed your ghost tour around the better known parts of the ancient city of York but bear in mind that this is by no means an exhaustive account. Our intention is to expand on the contents of Haunted York in future editions and for this we need your help. If you've had a spectral encounter in York, or if you have any knowledge of ghosts that haven't been covered in these pages, let us know. Any of the contact information at the beginning of the book will suffice and the more details the better.

Thanks must go to Rachel Lacy for the foreword.
Rachel is York's 'Ghost Finder General' and also a Paranormal Historian. She runs the Paranormal and Spectral Investigations (PSI) group which has been going since 2003 and is also involved in the York Ghost Festival. For more information see page 53 and go to:
www.psi-chicks.co.uk